SÔNG I SING

Sông I Sing

POEMS

BAO PHI

COFFEE HOUSE PRESS

MINNEAPOLIS 2011

COPYRIGHT © 2011 Bao Phi
AUTHOR PHOTOGRAPH © Charissa Uemura
COVER + BOOK DESIGN Coffee House Press
COVER ART © Binh Danh

Coffee House Press books are available to the trade through our primary distributor, Consortium Book Sales & Distribution, www.cbsd.com or (800) 283-3572. For personal orders, catalogs, or other information, write to: info@coffeehousepress.org.

Coffee House Press is a nonprofit literary publishing house. Support from private foundations, corporate giving programs, government programs, and generous individuals helps make the publication of our books possible. We gratefully acknowledge their support in detail in the back of this book. To you and our many readers around the world, we send our thanks for your continuing support.

Good books are brewing at www.coffeehousepress.org

LIBRARY OF CONGRESS CATALOGING-IN-PUBLICATION DATA
Phi, Bao, 1975–
Søng I sing : poems / by Bao Phi.
p. cm.
ISBN 978-1-56689-279-7 (alk. paper)
I. Title.
PS3566.H467 66 2011
811´.54—DC22
2011019841

3 5 7 9 8 6 4 2
Printed in the United States

for my Asian American people

1

2 The Nguyễns

3

4

The street was my cinema,
and I had free admission.

—LAC SU

For Us

From the mud of the Mekong to the bones of the Mississippi

From the dusty winds of Manzanar to the glowing scars of Hiroshima

From the sun in Bombay to the moon in Alaska

From the mists of the Himalayas to the ash of Volcano

From the hills of Laos to the openmouthed mic in St. Paul

From the streets of Seoul to the sidewalks of Tehrangeles

From California shores to New York corner stores

This is for us, my people, who carry the song of burning sugarcane in our lungs
Exhaling spirits with smoky spines
My people, who dig beneath sea foam with salted eyes
To exhume schools of ghosts
Lost from the boats.

This is for you, Celestial, Oriental, Asian, Asian Pacific American,
Woman, Man, Queer, broke, collegiate, young old gook, spitting chink,
Dog-eating dothead, faggot bitch slope,

Our beautiful black hair sticky from colliding with
Sugarcoated glass ceilings,
The ones voted most likely to assimilate
Asians: the other white meat
Bleached by color-blind lies
Buying DKNY and Calvin Klein
So our own bodies are gentrified

I

Bedecked in sweatshop swooshes
Resurfacing from under a pile
Of the white man's dirty laundry
To model our minority
Cutting our eyelids to be blind to beauty
Atkins-ing our way to a rice-free waistline
Shoving fingers down the throats of ancestors
To see what comes up.

This is for you, taught to believe in magic
Just not our own
Mistaking appeasement for peace
And selling out for maturity
While they box our geography
And sell it in bougie boutiques
Our culture quite profitable
But can somebody tell me
How our culture can be hip
And yet our people remain invisible?

Divisible individuals
This ghosthood of honorary whiteness
Miss Saigon-ing our way
Into the pale arms of con men

This is for you, twisting our names
Into bleached demons so foreign tongues
Could invoke them
Mastering our own blondspeak scrabbletalk
This scored mishmash of grab-bag didactics
Cringing at the sound of our mother tongue's syllables
This is for you, who use our split lungs as divining rods
To find the flow of our lost languages.

This is for you, whose homes are turned upside down
While men and women debate the sorrows of war
Safe from the scars of barbed wire
For you, whose lands are painted in smoke and bone
Neon bullets ripping thru green
Your heart the same shape
As the hole you buried your family in.

This is for you, whose sons and daughters picked up a gun
And wore a flag for the price of college tuition,
As your war stories fell under the noise of the machines
You operate to keep food on the table.

This is for you, shapeshifting evil, taking whatever form
They need for you to be the next enemy
Only loved when you can be used,
Asian people,
Only loved when you can be used.

This is for you, food-stamp-handed, banks bent over microchips
On conveyer belts, bodies bent from sleeping on buses
Hands like crumpled parchment
From washing dishes
Microphones ablaze with poetry
And song
Drunk off of friendship, struggling tongues
Faking our way through karaoke.

This is for you, the sugar of your love,
The kinship of cupped hands
The riddles in our hair
Which we pull out to make sure it's still black
Because we can't trust our mirrors anymore

3

This is for you, for all of you, who still don't know
How beautiful you are
This is for you, for all of you, who still don't know
How beautiful you are
This is for those of us who run our fingers down
Each other's faces
And swear
That no one
Is ever gonna steal our beauty away from us again.

This is for you
Who wiped the milk
Of honorary whiteness from your lips
And asked
Got Self?

My people, we are a song that we can never stop singing against the silence
My people, we are a song that we can never stop singing against the silence

This is for you, this is for má and bố,
For the family you got kicked out of,
For the street you cipher on
From the green terraces
That stack up in your dreams.

This is for the first time your curled your hand
Into a fist and understood who your enemy was
This is for the first time you picketed
The first time you sent money back to a cousin
In the motherland
This is for the first time you amplified
Your story.

We are not dandelions, weeds they uproot
To cleanse their fantasy gardens
And get their hands dirty in our soil
We are sunflowers, a blazing field
Of yellow-petal skins and brown eyes
Standing together.

This is for you,
For your yellow-brown skin
This is for you
For your black hair
This is for that beautiful mirror
I see in your eyes
This is for you
This is for you
My people
This
Is for
Us.

FOBulous

FOBulous

Fresh Off the Boat
Follower Of Buddha

Fucking Old Bastards
(and their sons too)
Fucking Over Browns

a Fetish Only for yellow Bedfellows
Frequent Oriental Brothels
Fugitives On Board
knew ancient Chinese secrets to Fantastic Orgasm Benefits

Funny Oriental Boys
feel like Fucked Overlooked Bachelors
Footbinding Outmoded Barbarians
Burying Our Feelings —
Frigid Oppositional Bookworms

Fascists Often Bungle
Fate Often Boomerangs

Fat Overweight B-boys
Failed Olympic Boxers
gay or straight — Femme Or Butch

Families Often Barbecue
sip Fizzy Orange Beverages
while screaming Finally! Our Bulgogi!

Forecast Our Brotherhood and Sisterhood
and Broadcast on Our Feet,
on FOB-Operated Bicycles

Get the word out
Forsaking Our Blessings
has been greatly exaggerated
My people
never
Forget Our Beauty.

Waiting for a Cyclo in the Hood

Twenty-Sixth Street, a one-way,
flows by my house, keeps going right
out of the hood before spilling into
Uptown: fertile delta of the young,
disturbingly hip, rich by no fault of their own,
nothing to do on a Saturday night but be beautiful.
I sit on the curb, far from lovely,
empty pocket's distance from rich,
wishing I knew
which way to go.
Back in Viet Nam I could
shout for a cyclo, hold up a fist of small đồng
peel each dollar from the tension of my hand
and let them fly away to the Dopplar Effect,
one by one,
scream the words to Prince's *1999* in two languages
and not once look behind me to see
if the driver was whispering:
this street is one way, I can't take you back
to where you came from, no matter how many American
dollar bills you give up
to the wind.

You Bring Out the Vietnamese in Me
after Sandra Cisneros, "You Bring Out the Mexican in Me"

Tôi la một ngư ờ'i Vietnamese / Bilingual / Poetry / MC
you want to thank me well / không có chi
let me take you for a ride / of my refugeography
if your mama could cook you know she'd make a batch of me
nasty catastrophes / O'i trờ'i O'i / Fatality/ See / Bao Phi
la một ngư ờ'i bâ't lịch sự' / Well, excuse me
I say one for Asian / Two for American / And three for love
you may say hot like whoa / but I say hot like phở.
Phở real. Phở life. Phở-king Phở-nomenal.

Because you bring out the Vietnamese in me.

The waiting fireball.
The suntanned angel on a rice terrace.
The black-haired miracle.

You
bring out the Vietnamese in me,
the salted yellow boat-child and military brat on an airplane in me,
the tracer-bullet-eyed Buddhist who gets presents on Christmas in me,

the nuở'c mắm, cà phê sũa đá, mangoes and mang cut,
mít and coconut, sugar-dried strawberries in Đà Lạt
and sweet xá xíu stains Asian American in me,
the dry-season-heat hearted and black eyebrow as floodgate
for monsoon eyes in me,

the three stripes like Sông Hu'o'ng blood
and Sông Mê Kông spine in me,

the Phillips to Cedar Square projects to Frogtown
in a powder-blue used Datsun blaring Depeche Mode in me,
the whole can of Aqua Net in my hair, switchblade in my right pocket,
razor boxcutter in my left,
baseball bat in the backseat
gun in the glove compartment
in case you want to fuck
with the refugee in me,

You,
yes you,
whiplash of black hair
and your heart a rose of flame,

You bring out the Vietnamese in me,

The Agent Orange Kool-Aid drinker and burner of government cheese in me,
the sharpener and painter of fingernails
sipping ginger ale in plastic snap champagne glasses
at Prom Center while twisting tornado tango fandangos
in mango-colored suits and white ruffled shirts in me,
the I'm not gonna talk about love
I'm gonna be it in me,

You bring out
the college degree prodigy thug in me,
the communist / republican / I wish there were more
Vietnamese progressives around
in me,
the I'll change the oil filter my goddamn self and
blow the money I saved on lottery tickets in me,
the incense and cigarettes and white clothes at the funeral in me,

You bring out the Vietnamese in me,
circling on the Lê Lợi boulevard loop
with a thousand other young Saigon Viets,
blinking taillights of Honda Dream II mopeds like flicked
cigarette butts and laughter
like wind in our faces,

You bring out the Vietnamese in me,
the *Mùa thu lá bay*
and *Sài Gòn đẹp lắm Sài Gòn ơi, Sài Gòn ơi, Sài Gòn ơi,* —
the firefly in a lee kum kee jar,
the terraced voice,
the sugarcane chunks in plastic bags,
the weak beer and strong cigarettes,
the Fanta soda toothpick slinger,
the yogurt-based soft drinks,
the sudden death syndrome,

You bring out
The leaky boat that won't sink
The family photo clutched tight to a chest
When all the rest of the world burns

You
bring out the Vietnamese
in me

tell my life by reading my palm
and you'll find calluses

that's why love is at home
in my tired muscles

and burns under my eyelids
while I sleep,

men, women, soldiers of every color
have walked into my life,
left burning-flag-shaped scars,
left ghosts shaped like my family,
left me
for dead,

I was the one who survived to love you.
Even if you save me, I won't thank you.

I love to save myself from myself,
I love so these things become me without ruling me,
I love you
because you bring out the Vietnamese in me,

You

Yes, you

Yes, you.

The Nguyễns

*Who am I? You know who I am. Or you think you do . . . I'm
the one you call Gook. I'm the one you don't see at all — we all
look alike. I'm the one you see everywhere —
we're taking over the neighborhood . . . There. That's it. I've
said it. Now can I go?*

—JULIE OTSUKA

The Nguyễns

Mỹ says that her family teases her for having thick boy legs but really she is the perfect autumn night sky trapped in a woman's body. When she laughs you feel night wind blowing through leaves making them blush and change color — when she laughs you feel the breath of stars and lunar eclipses under her eyelids.

California has shortened his name to Cali and he is from Portland, Oregon. He works in the video game industry doing voice-over work, which he calls voice acting. He never questions why the characters he's doing voices for are always the bad guys. At night he dreams that he's Godzilla, stomping blond heroes beneath his giant lizard feet.

Vina has spent the day cleaning penguin shit off the rocks at the zoo while daydreaming of being a *Paris By Night* star, and now it's two a.m. and she's haunting the puke-lit twenty-four-hour grocery store like a famished Japanese horror flick ghost tapping her fingers onto melons and eating grapes without paying for them.

Johnny dances to songs he half understands, his hairstyle is one and a half decades out of style and he really should button up his silk shirt maybe just a little bit more but he's just spent ten hours under cars fixing them up for people who assumed his gook ass was sabotaging their good ole American steel as much as he was fixing them so who are you to tell him anything while he dances?

Việt is, as her name suggests, Vietnamese as fuck. She only eats Vietnamese food, watches Vietnamese films, speaks fluent Vietnamese, reads Vietnamese literature, hangs out with Vietnamese people, only dates Vietnamese people, and is bisexual so she can be attracted to twice as many Vietnamese people. She drives a Korean car — which is not Vietnamese but as close as she can get. She sold you your cell phone and she thinks that you are stupid.

Dotty tattoos Hai Bà Trưng on her shoulders in the hopes that those legendary heroic sisters will help her shoulder the weight, she publishes zines and shouts perfect English into bullhorns and signs her name on so many different petitions that the causes all seem to blur together while she wonders how her family is doing since they kicked her out of the house.

Huey's real name is Huế and he tells you he may be a descendant of the Nguyễn kings but he's all Queen, baby, recognize. He's been on his feet all day at the casino sliding cards like ninja stars across green felt tables under old Asian faces. He wants to forget the look on those faces, faces like his father mother grandfather grandmother as their dreams of fortune crash with the gentle sound of cards flipping onto their bellies.

Bác Trâm doesn't reply when you say cám ơn for the bowl of phở. It's just her in this place, from nine a.m. to midnight, so it's her right to take your money and give you your basil mint bean sprout lime platter and hate your guts from the safety of the kitchen. One night when she's bored she'll tell you she hasn't been back to Viet Nam since her husband died, she'll ask you if you have a job, she'll ask you if your girlfriend is white or Vietnamese as if those are the only two choices in the world.

Linda's Vietnamese name is Thùy, her daddy is a Buddhist and her momma's a Catholic and tonight she's holding up a rum and coke and toasting to nondenominational sin. No she would not like to dance with your goofy ass but thanks for asking, she is in this club to be seen and to chain-smoke American Spirits like the burning embers are beacons to paradise dangling just out of reach at the tip of her nose

and Vĩnh sits with her and though he wishes he were a cigarette filter so he could know the stain of her lipstick kiss, he says nothing, he has given up on love but has not given up smoking or Long Island ice teas and tomorrow he'll wake up with a hangover and, though fully clothed, he

will find many dollar bills stuck into his underpants and he won't
remember how they got there.

Last name, Nguyễn, all of them
they're not related
but they're more related than any of them will ever know.

Their last name is not Nguyễn,
it's Trần, it's Bùi, Phan, Đoàn, Huỳnh,
and they are pissed off that this poem suggests they are not Vietnamese
just cuz their last name is not Nguyễn.

They sell cars in Orange County, they sell shoes in Queens,
hustle from White Bear Lake to Frogtown, Minnesota,
they drawl their way into your heart through Virginia and Texas,
lost everything to Katrina
fight for their lives every day in Boston
bake mango cheesecakes in Oakland and San Francisco,
where they live affects how they feel about the weather
and whether or not they say yes when you ask them to step out of their
front door
for some karaoke or late-night Chinese.

They sneak bánh mì into bad movies and they don't see themselves on
the silver screen enough to dream about being up there someday. They
gamble too much and they smoke too much and they look great playing
billiards and their feet hurt and they've been working all day and they
are none of your motherfucking business.

They are one story for every Việt body, one song for every voice that
sings or otherwise, every Vietnamese name is like a tattoo we all wear
proud, a burst of color dug deep to dance
across our skins.

Love, Angel, Music, Baby
CATHY NGUYỄN WRITES TO GWEN STEFANI

I know, Nguyễn is Vietnamese but, you know,
Japanese, Vietnamese, tomato,
tomahtoe.

When I went back to Viet Nam everyone saw my straight-cut bangs
and expertly ripped clothes, bowed and said konichiwa
so even my own people saw me as Japanese, doesn't that count
for anything?

Gwen, *guuuuurl*, I know we'd get along well — I had a tattoo when I
        was a cheerleader
that made my dark skin in my all-white Midwestern suburb
stand out like *grrrrrr*

I was fearless, you understand, I was up in your face —
but not too much,
the spiked belts had to be the right color,
coordinate
you know what I mean, Gwen, no attitude that you can't
put on a credit card

So give me a chance, I've been practicing my sneer in the mirror,
curling my lip up at my reflection
so I can unleash it on those I see fit for my exotic disdain
I can hide my chinky-eyed squint
behind chunky smoky sunglasses at least as wide
as yours

Domo Origato, Missus Roboto, I'll sign any contract you want
change Nguyễn to Nagasaki, or Love, Angel, Music, Baby

I'll lip-sync my new name
curl my lip into fake accessory of an accent
if you take me in a limo to riot grrrrrl glam revolution
I promise I won't speak English
when you take away my name.

Vu Nguyễn's Revenge
NGUYỄN, VU — SACRAMENTO

Fuck you, Chavis Johnson, for pushing me down in ninth grade
and calling me gook
while the diverse population of our high school's
multicultural laughter slammed flat like your pale palm
against my chest.

Fuck you for having no fear even when my hate sucked hot
air into a vortex and my breathing shaped my lungs to knives
even if you were a foot taller and outweighed me by 100 pounds
and your haircut crowning your square head
cost $50 more than mine.

Fuck you for doing it all in front of Monica Nguyễn
who always had a crush on you, who you once joked
must be related to me because we're both Nguyễns
and we laughed,
me, because I didn't want to get my ass kicked,
she, because she wanted to be loved.

Fuck you for calling me gook and beating me down
in front of her drowned brown eyes
that never looked into mine again
you bragged two years later
that she gave up her virginity
after you took her to see *Miss Saigon*

Fuck you for breaking her heart
even though she took your side
and made fun of me for playing Dungeons and Dragons
though now I hear she lives in the suburbs reading *Harry Potter*
married a white man not at all like you
(probably fantasizes about fucking Legolas
and is addicted to Percocet)

Fuck you for not being around
after I sold my rare first-edition *Deities and Demigods* book
Cthulhu mythos and all,
and bought a gym membership with the money
to bench-press my way into my own mirror

Fuck you for *not* trying to push me *after* the $60 a month
tae kwon do lessons, the gorging on red meat to gain pounds,
made my Buddhist mom cry cuz I spent every night
praying to Jesus for a late growth spurt
that finally shot me six inches closer to heaven
(thank you Jesus)

Where is your wheat-haired crown now,
where is your Made-in-America tongue:
a slide of spit to take me back to where I came from
now that I am ready to show you
show you
where I come from
Where are you now when I am the Goliath,
the chink-eyed Greek statue
who beat up a hundred white guys in a hundred bars
just for looking like you,
went to jail three times just so I could brag about it
my hands clenching and unclenching
wanting to haunt your neck

Where are you now, pale dwarf, comic-book villain,
where are you now when my hands,
riddled with righteous calluses, ache for you,
when I am the kung fu hero come back to the hamlet
for revenge, ready to Ong Bak your ass
in front of a cheering throng of yellow-brown people?

Why can't you be here now, calling me gook in a parking lot
or screaming from a car window
so that I can chase you
so that my anger can be the mushroom cloud
that scars you and your family for life,
so that I can be the one to stand still
and watch
you
run,

so that I can ask, finally,
why the world is always ready for your kind of hate
but never mine?

Fuck you, oh good lord, fuck you, Chavis Johnson,
Biblical locust swarms eat your cock, Chavis Johnson
sudden tsunamis drown your gated suburbs, Chavis Johnson,
corrupt judges deport you back to Scandinavia, Chavis Johnson.
If God won't damn people like you
I will
so damn you, Chavis Johnson
for not being here,
now,
when I'm ready for you,
with curled fist

and stump of a war scream
to pummel you into a shape
you
never
wanted to become.

Fusion

NGUYỄN, KAYLEE — CHICAGO

Do you know why food is like love?
Because it is sooooo much better
than it needs to be.

Instead of a dirty shriveled root in water
it's walleye in ginger and scallion.

Instead of dry stale bread
it's red flecks of chili in orange oil.

Food is like love, because it is more than just sustenance.

It began with the tracks of roaches in fine red Kool-Aid dust,
stray ramen spice packets,
a dry block of government cheese blackened, not melted.
Cans of Beefaroni
I fought my grandfather for,
the multitude of perch and crappie my father caught
in the pond by the highway
without a license,
and the rat that crawled out of our toilet and
ate my little sister's butter cookie
given to us by our Lutheran sponsor.

My first recipe given to me the day my mother slapped me
when I read in the newspaper
about how Vietnamese refugees
were stealing cats and dogs and eating them
and I asked my mom if it was the granulated gray bits
of a puppy in our evening's cháo.

It continued in college, when I cooked for every eggroll appreciation
day, where everyone wanted
the flavor of culture
without the rotted scent of racism.
This is where white people began to think
I was one of them,
they saw
what they thought was a good Asian girl
who didn't need to be reminded of her place
because she kept herself there.

I paid my dues in a restaurant where the gray swinging doors between
        us yellow-brown
cooks was like a border to the lily-white linen skin of the waitstaff,
who claimed to be working class and poo-poo'd any allegations
that a white restaurant cooking fake Asian Latino food
could be racist
drinking beer while we stayed behind to mop the floors,
the white dude who said, "sure, I may be a little sexist, but I'm not a racist,"
as he slapped the ass of the one
Thai waitress.

Now, I am a chef
to customers.
I am a cook
to the people I love.

See me slit a green onion
from the thin green flag to the thick bottom white root

See me dirty my hands in ginger root whiskers
my own fingers
uprooted from homeland

See the razor dance I perfect
with Japanese steel and the translucent
whisper of sashimi

and they see fusion.

East, West, they say. Buddha's delight.

But they don't smell the fish sauce
on the tips of my lapels,
or the grilled dry-squid stink
that kids made fun of,
the greased fried rice
that made me a freak at the lunch table.

All this time people put what it took
to make me who I am,
to make what they put in their mouths,
and no one asks me —

well, anything.

So then, let me tell you,
that when I see the wilted attempts at vegan Vietnamese cuisine
made by white people in co-ops
I think of Britney Spears in an áo dài.

Let me tell you that the white people
can choke to death on their lychee martinis
and if the white waitstaff try to express solidarity with us
brown folks stained with the labor of the kitchen,
tell them they had a chance,
and they already picked their side.

Let me tell you I have dreamed of hunting them
with machetes,
with AK-47s, with M16s, spears
and blowguns, bow and arrow,
switchblades
and wooden stakes diseased by excrement.

Clubbing them over the head
with smallpox blankets, chains and manacles,
bottles of whiskey,
with empty McDonalds cups
and spent shell casings,
baskets of fruit coated by cancerous pesticides.

And in these dreams I roar up the fires beneath the melting pot
tie them to the steam tables
stick scallions into their ears
slice eyelash-thin pieces of ginger
onto them as they scream,
splash soy
on darkening, crisping skin
playfully fight
over the rice at the bottom of the kettle
playfully fight
for the check
and let the elders
eat the eyeballs
right out of their skull.

And in my dreams I say

if you don't like to be eaten
the way you like to be served

just remember
you were the ones
who gave us
the recipe.

And when I wake up
I tell the people I love:
give me the hungriest night of your life
and I swear
I'll burn down this entire goddamn city
to cook for you.

Mercy

NGUYỄN, JOHN — ROTC, IRAQ

Let my father know it is not
for his blood
that I fight this war.

His decision, made in Saigon.
Mine, made at a recruiting table in an L.A. high school

Let him know that his hands, which once cradled guns
in another war,
are not my hands.

Let his friends know the difference,
at least to us,
between a communist and an Iraqi
and understand why he won't speak about me.

Let my mother know one day where she
does not fear violence an ocean away
where the body and home
are not always in a dance
toward fracture.

Let my little hippie sister's letters to me, telling me it's not my fault
I was sent to this unjust war, be true,
at least in the eyes of God.
Concerning my little brother
who stabbed a white man in San Jose for calling him a chink
let the judge presiding over his case
know that what my brother did,
he did in the name of war.

Let the last cradle of my tender vessel
not be this godforsaken Humvee.

Let this boredom, this blessed boredom,
easily fill that thin space between my finger
and the trigger.

If bullets should fly, let the air pounding from
my lungs as I run be my song.

Let my affection for the people here, for the children here,
be real, not sweetened by Nestle or Coca-Cola
or plastic toys Made in China.

Let them know I am trying to understand
no matter what I say or do,
it is never enough
because they never asked for this.

Let me not tear apart a people, a country, causing Iraqi food to
become the nouvelle cuisine in twenty-five years back home,
like they did to my people —
let me not become my father, and my son or daughter, myself,
wandering the wavering borders made by someone else.

Let me ask this and mean it,
Though I'm the one holding the gun.

Let the globe on the desk be mightier than the grenade.

The soldier, who looked at me and snorted, *gooks killing ragheads,*
that would make a great video game, let him know a hatred
he never asked for and cannot reason with, and let him die with it
choking his sleep, and let it pass
onto his children and haunt his children's children,
without mercy.

The Eminem wannabe Marine, who when freestyling in the cipher in our barracks squeaked *me love you long time*, saw me scowl at him, and who the night after left a bullet on my pillowcase with a pair of tiny lips scratched into the casing, let me not be tempted to be first, to beat him to the finish line of the race that he and his kind set up, let me not be tempted to line up the promise in the eye of my M4 to the back of his bleached blond hair, let me not chain lightning from my finger through the hollow echo in the valley of the chamber through to the domed pellet of steel that would become his whistling reaper, let me not be the first, of he and I

to play God. Let me not pull the trigger on his story. But let everyone know that I could have.

Let me pronounce the last names of the curly-haired Filipina twins in the next platoon correctly, even as they pronounce Nguyễn as best they can.

Let every poor brown, black, yellow soul who signed up for college tuition have children who grow up to be NBA stars drafted for millions out of high school.

Let me have the courage to erase the names of the dead
from my cell phone.

Let my lover, in our most private darkness, know, that when I tell her
you have a Quixotic pussy
except
that your pussy tilts windmills —
let her know, that I mean
that she, the all of her,
has a gravitational pull
and I am only a man
helpless in her current
I am swept in her undertow
and I drown
gladly.

Let her know, as the Lord is my witness, that I have confessed
to doubting God
but I have never doubted
her.

If we mirror one another then let us be both our homelands —
she, the jagged edge of California, and I her reflection, the jigsaw
coast of Viet Nam, or one, the other,

and let no one say I fought this war to make a better world
for our unborn children.

Let them know that I mean the first Persian Gulf,
let them know I mean Viet Nam, and Korea,
and the bombs that made blossoms of Hiroshima and Nagasaki,
let them know I mean every man that will call me gook
every man that will slap my sister behind a closed door
let them know I mean police beating down Cambodian kids
in the park
and people who make fun of my mother using welfare checks
at the supermarket
let them know I mean my father screaming in nightmares
and ghetto neighbors who call my parents gook
when walking by their front yard
Let them know I mean my uncles drinking themselves to death
and aunties losing life savings at blackjack and
white hunters killing Hmong in Wisconsin
and yes, let them know I mean this, here, now, Iraq,
when I say
Fuck this war.

Changeling

NGUYỄN, CUTTY — BOSTON

with thanks to Christopher Chinn

Cutty as in crazy gook bitch will cut you,
cracking gum in the shadows of hi-rise ghetto-in-the-sky
before newspapers were spread on shag carpet
for that evening's curry dinner.
In the dark, are her fingernails
shiny enough to be mistaken for blades?

Cutty as in Cutie, China Doll taking up
too much space at the Oriental Food market
stacking boxes of interethnic ramen
stealing cans of Mr. Coffee during fifteen-minute breaks
ignores the stares from white men with rings
on their fingers —
and in the parking lot,
I fought for your people in the war, bitch, you owe me.

Cutty as in Cuttlefish, or more accurately squid,
mực her daddy would heat up for her on the greased plug-in grill
that would blow fuses if the microwave
was used at the same time, that stink the neighbors
complained about, along with the perfume of
fish sauce, the pre-crunk of Viet new wave,
that smell and sound, the gooks have come,
watch out for your pets,
American tragedy turned best seller
between the covers of a book.

Cutty as in Củ Chi, traitor in a tunnel
rising snakelike

from a hole you never expected in the earth,
innocent dirt you could turn your back to
suddenly now the slant-eyed succubus
stabbing you with a chopstick she took from the bun
in her hair.

Cutty as in never quietly, but seldom heard, as in, Cutty as in who gives
a fuck what you think anyway, Cutty as in everything I need to be, as in,
Cutty is not my name
it should be obvious but you never asked.

Zeke Got a Zorro Signature
NGUYỄN, EZEKIEL — NEW YORK CITY

Ezekiel Nguyễn got a Zorro signature —
every time he signs
his zigzag name
it's like the letters are breakdancers
with busted arms and legs
scrawled on the sides of telephone booths,
splintered bus stop benches,
and bounced checks

Ezekiel has seen too many Hong Kong flicks
daydreams of sliding across the kitchen floor
instead of mopping it
the hot steam like fog machines
for dramatic entry
packs two gats one gun
for each of your lungs
fuck death
fuck around and that's your breath

Ezekiel also answers when you call out
Zeke or Z
when his name is shortened to match his scar —
lightning down his left cheek
legend has it
Agent Orange burned him in the womb like Shazam
legend has it
he crawled as a baby through barbed wire
to cut his cheek a new smile
legend has it
a switchblade cut that bolt
held by a Lao gangster for looking at his girl in a pool hall

he says he doesn't even see it no more
when he looks in the mirror
he says he's so pretty he distracts himself
from it
that scar runs like a signature down his face
he gets tired of his own legend
long before you do.

And the Waves

NGUYỄN, KATRINA — NEW ORLEANS

We thought the worst was over, then the water came.

No, I can't begin there. Yes I am Vietnamese, yes I am from New Orleans.

Still?

I was born in New Orleans, and Katrina is not my real name. Well, it was not the name I was born with. "Walking on Sunshine"? I listened to it all the time when I was a little girl, and I thought Katrina was such a pretty name. You know she's from New Orleans too?

If I tried to teach you how to pronounce my given name,
you'd know why I go by Katrina.

I had a donut shop —   *Walking*
                                              on
                                              Donuts

Yeah, my customers didn't get it either, it seems no one can see my face and skin and think of music.

But every new customer who came through the door was ready for a story, my story, and when they asked me where I'm from, I could tell them exactly, right here, New Orleans, in my own shop when Vietnamese shrimpers, Mexican and Chinese restaurant workers,
black and white dockworkers,
the Arab greengrocers who called me their friend,
the two Native American men who worked at UPS,
everybody came in
for coffee, donuts,

37

and for the story buried in a name
after I told my tale no one asked, *where are you really from?*

They have these shirts now: "Katrina Gave Me a Blow Job I'll Never Forget," and "Katrina: Bitch Blew the Whole City."

Now people will ask me, again, where I got my name.

There was an elderly Vietnamese woman who survived on her own for weeks by catching fish out of the muck and drying them on the windshields of half-submerged cars.

A couple days after the big flood my friends and I paid tribute to her. Gloria found some lipstick floating around a few blocks from a flooded Walgreens and Mai salvaged some hip waders from her father's fishing gear. We put on that purple lipstick and those hip waders and danced on top of half-drowned cars for a while, laughing and hooting.

I wish I could say we did what we set out to do. But we didn't. Even as we danced and tried to celebrate being alive and kicking, I could feel my teeth, hard and unmoving, beneath any smile I could manage.

We were here too. There, I said it. There were Catholic priests who confessed to one another in Vietnamese for the sin of stealing boats to save lives. There were Buddhist monks who smoked cigarettes and played guitar to relieve the stress of wet drowning death and every soggy heavy life you were able to lift above the water. There were tattooed men and women eating crawdads on heaping plates with hot sauce and cold beer and singing Vietnamese songs.

Why weren't we on the news? Not even after they wanted to build a garbage dump smack dab in the middle of our community?

It's like this country only allows us one grief at a time. Your people, you had that war thing. That's all you get. Shut. The fuck. Up.

Can I talk about my parents? How they worked as shrimpers until the KKK came like ghosts starched stiff, rifles pointing to God in their arms like crucifixes, threatening their lives for working too hard?

Now you want to save me. When I'm pretty and tragic, the white horses start to stampede in the distance. What if I told you that, through all this water, I don't even know what salvation looks like. If you are my salvation on the other side of the glass on this gold fishbowl, how will I be able to tell a helping hand from a fishhook?

I mark time by the waterlines on the few houses that aren't destroyed. I see stray cats who miraculously survived the flood and I want to scream to everyone that we are not eating them. I want to put on lipstick and dance anywhere dry and high. I want to make enough donuts in my ruined shop to feed every yellow, brown, black, red, white person in New Orleans, a Vietnamese superhero dusted in flour, wrapped in a cape reeking of the luxurious heavy smell of deep-fat fryers, a halo glowing golden like a reflection of my skin stained earth-brown with coffee.

Katrina, Katrina. I've never heard my own name more often, in the news and on the street. But no one sees me.

You don't understand? Let me tell you, my name is Katrina, yes, I am Vietnamese, and yes, I am from New Orleans. We thought the worst was over. Then the water came.

The Nguyễn Twins Find Adoration
in the Poetry World

1. JOAN NGUYỄN

her poems are willows bending
over ponds her parents died in,
an orange being peeled by a leprous prostitute's hands,
Vietnamese sentences she never fails to translate
in italics
for *Ploughshares, The Kenyon Review,*
her book *Muscular Treaties* won the Pushcart, the Yale Younger
Writers,
the safe ethnic poet award.

She and her boyfriend Chad Kaufman
have a fine
but modest house that seems to be held up
by overstuffed bookcases.
At the reception, she stands by dull silver plates
smeared by unpronounceable cheeses
as smiling people say nice things
to "the Vietnamese poet and her American boyfriend"
one woman leans over
and whispers with sugary envy and cocked brow
"you're going to have such beautiful kids!"

There is only one other Asian there,
Ms. Clementine Chow-Wyatt
stuck teaching freshman comp for years,
looks at Joan like she is a land mine
planted on the steps
up to the Caucasian tower

Joan read Clementine's book, found it quaint,
unsophisticated, minor
she mouths *Nguyễn-Kaufman* silently
as she watches Ms. Chow-Wyatt
stand like a garland of barbed wire
around the cheese plate
poking at the last bit of Afuega'l Pitu.

2. JESUS NGUYỄN

his poems are system fascist overthrow racism working class
immigrant rights male feminist Mumia Mumia fuck Bush motherfucker
    motherfucker
after his three minutes on Def Poetry Jam the crowd
jumps out of their seats and proclaims *Jesus!*

At the after-party his CD *Get Middle Class or Die Tryin'*
sells so well, no one calls him out
for mispronouncing almost every Vietnamese word
that he uses in his poetry (all three of them)

Everyone in the joint is black, Latino/a,
some white dudes
who talk like Michael Rapaport,
everybody got a flyer
everybody looking for digits of someone
a couple rungs down the ladder of oppression from them
you know what they say,
the darker the berry the sweeter the injustice
brother, can I romanticize your oppression?

When he's drunk enough Jesus will tell whomever in
his flock that will listen that he flunked intro to poetry

because he told his professor
you white people are just mad that us people of color
came up with making sense as a poetic device
before you did

One other Asian is there
whom Jesus calls Multicultural Man
comes up and gives Jesus a hug
though he compared his poems to unlit Molotov cocktails
on a radical leftist message board

Multicultural Man drags Jesus into a freestyle cipher
misty spit flies from beatboxing mouths
as staccato syllables dance like
fashionable danger
no one can tell apart.

NoTown, USA
NGUYỄN, DINH — NEAR LINCOLN, NEBRASKA

Even the post office has no gossip,
he doesn't receive mail
or send. He showed up three years ago, his hair all cut off,
in a '94 Celica that puffed clouds out of the exhaust bigger than
the ones over the highway.
Found work as a cook in the only Chinese restaurant in town,
fried rice, chicken wings, sweet and sour pork are the top orders.
He washes dishes. He doesn't really cook, he burns.

On break sometimes he snaps bits of kindling-dry beef jerky into a cup
of ramen and calls it white-trash phở, as close as he can get in this town.

Everyone is more familiar with the back of his shaved head
than his face.
No one asks but everybody wonders.
Is he some naughty monk banished from his monastery
because his kung fu was too lusty?

Some wild-brained escaped lunatic
who sees pink rabbits and blue elephants?

Is he from a war with whispered secrets from a country with
an often mispronounced name immortalized in immigrant
literature and Oliver Stone films?

Or could it be he's just a man, in this town whose name
the tourists always just forget,
just a man who won't tell you a goddamn thing
because that would be against the point and the point.
is to be forgotten,

because he knows that everyone tries their best
and fails
and he has come here beyond eyesight
so that every day he can
defeat himself quietly, in peace.

Dotty Nguyễn's Plea upon the Day Her Mother Accused Her of Being a Commie and Kicked Her Out of the Family

NGUYỄN, DOTTY — DALLAS

Ask me to scrape the tattoos of the Hai Bà Trưng off my shoulders
with steel wool

Ask me to put down my bullhorn and stop marching with Chicanos
and Asians and the multitude of colored skins down the streets of L.A.

Ask me again how it's possible to have a paying job when you work at
something called a nonprofit

Ask me to write the Patriot Act in colored balloon graffiti letters across
the brick fortress walls of the INS building

Ask me to write more letters to my brother, your son, as he waits
cradling a rifle in his arms in Iraq

Ask me to speak fluent Vietnamese while I'm not at a restaurant, to
recite passages of *Truyện Kiều* from memory while rolling eggrolls
into tight cylinders so perfect they must be crammed tight into the hot
oil pan to keep from rolling

Ask me to save my money instead of going out to drink on the
weekends, tell me again why I shouldn't trust the bank and should
stash cash under my mattress

Ask me to take back the way you hid the food stamps by holding your
hand up like a fan of shame at the checkout line

Ask me to stop kissing other girls in public, ask me to wear pants that
don't have holes in them, ask me for fewer piercings and ask me to
rewind time and never get that nose ring

45

Ask me to add and subtract rather than divide, to never stop being fascinated with frogs and bugs the way I was when I was a little girl with glasses so thick that brother told me not to look at the sun too long or the rays would sear my eyeballs right out of their sockets

Ask me for a mix CD that you would actually like, ask me to take you for lobster at either of the two Chinese restaurants you approve of, ask me to introduce my cousins to other nice Vietnamese boys and girls who are good looking and who have good jobs

Ask me to take back the fire that broke like waves onto everything our people knew to be green and living, ask me to take away the flap of skin that marks where the bullet passed through your body,

Ask me to take back your brother who stayed with the communists in the North and called you a whore for betraying your people

Ask me to take back the day they took your husband

Ask me to forget his face even when you can't,

Ask me to remember my name, and forget it,

Ask me anything, just don't ask me

To stop calling you my mother.

Cleats Crowned by Soil
NGUYỄN, UNITY — POWDERHORN PARK, MINNEAPOLIS
for the Third World Alliance Soccer Crew

Unity Nguyễn bought the least oppressive soccer shoes
she could find, the company promised
no sweatshop servitude stitched the leather.
Today she grinds the heel
into grass diamonded by dew
by the small man-made pond
in the park dubbed by locals to be inner-city dangerous.

Here *she* is the one who wants to be feared.

See her red jersey, Number 6, Sun Wen's number,
best goddamn player in the world she will tell you
like a flag of blood on a green field of war
Ask her if she's Chinese and she'll shrug
Unity knows what side she's on
Just like she knew
when the Chinese women played against the u.s. in 1999
Unity saw black hair, yellow-brown skin
roaring like a tidal wave of legs and feet
I don't have to be Chinese, she says, *I knew who to cheer for —*
just like she knew in 2002, when she raised her beer
for the Korean men, a blur of shoes and heartbeat drumming down grass
I ain't gotta be Korean, she says,
I know whose side I'm on.

Unity sees the ball and she runs,
lets her breath take her,
she hustles and stutter-steps past

Chicano/as, Indigenous, Africans, African Americans, Indians, Arabs,
        Chinese, Hmong,
who, without jerseys, are busboys, artists-activists, community workers,
nonprofit hustlers, investment bankers,
they work nail salons and rock mics and
in a few hours they will be friends and neighbors again
but not right now, goddamnit —
they are between her and glory.

She runs like her shoes are laced with
a million garment worker eyelashes,
past her daddy who told her to play tennis, a good civilized game
(not soccer, he says, like the dirty shoeless Lao and Cambodian kids at the park),
past ads of white suburban women fashionably liberated
in sweatshop swooshes
to
just do it,

past the haunting mouths taunting *gook, chink bitch, butch, dyke, communist,*
        feminaẓi,
how people can call you by so many names
yet see so little of you —
today she is too fast to hear those echoes

She belongs only to the sun, to the raw kicking earth
that buckles under her swift shadow —
her crown, the rings of soil on her cleats,
her lungs, wind,
her legs, the scissor of breath,
and this day, on this field, her life, her glory
is hers
to run to.

Prince among Men

NGUYỄN, QUINCY — NORTHSIDE, MINNEAPOLIS

Lyrics translated into Vietnamese by
Leilani ly-huơng Nguyễn and Mimi Nguyễn

đâu có muốn làm cho em buồn tênh
đâu có muốn làm cho em đau lòng

Why not purple velvet and lace instead of white leather jumpsuits studded
with sequins split by a river of hairy chest?

Why not, instead of a king, a Prince?

Especially for a boy named Quincy Nguyễn from Northside
when other boys his age deafened themselves with 50 Cent,
Christina Aguilera, Fallout Boy, and John Mayer,
Quince tacked the dog-eared sleeve of *Lovesexy* onto his wall
cuz the platter never left his turntable anyway

His eyelashes were winter branches, black and long,
his facial hair, immaculately groomed —
a beautiful boy
as if *Kiss Me Kiss Me Kiss Me*–era Robert Smith
had a love child with *Faith*-era George Michael
sure kids gave him shit but Quince had mastered
retorts using Prince lyrics, or

The zen of answering by not answering

OBSERVE!

Look at this freak man. Hey, you! Yeah you! The fuck, you Puerto Rican,
Chinese?

49

Let a woman be woman and a man a man.

What kind of answer is that? Don't you speak English, freak? You gay or something? WHAT, YOU A FUCKING FAGGOT OR SOMETHING?"

There's no sign I'm more compatible with.

Prince gave him the power,
secret to survival for small boys
odd when young yet destined for
futuresexy
the maze of the tongue
where fools get lost in lyric.

Quince also worked a five and dime
and so had his first choice at

used

fabulousness —

Among the frayed threads and too-long sleeves
he never asked if it cheapened him
to put on someone else's life —

at the second-hand store,

everything

has already been someone else's costume

Poppa bought him a used guitar
and begged his son, please, if you're going to sing and dress like a woman
could you learn some Patsy Cline, some Crystal Gayle,

his English not so good, but the stories in country music,
he could understand —

"I
Fall
To
Pieces"

What Vietnamese person doesn't understand that shit?

anh đâu có muốn làm cho em buồn tênh
anh đâu có muốn làm cho em đau lòng

One day when a mosaic of boys
called Quince sissy before turning into a symphony of punches and kicks
there was no music that could save him
in that whirlwind
that swirling spit funnel of fists mingled chink
foot to faggot
blood in the mouth
sissy queer gook
one back quivering
above the weeds in the sidewalk
one reed swaying
under a windmill
of limbs

How his father grabbed an oar from the garage
and wandered down Broadway asking every person he saw
ARE YOU THE ONE WHO BEAT UP MY SON?

While his father sought revenge never asked for,
Quince showers, sits at the mirror,
then puts needle to record,

bruises like oily puddles of water
he covers, foundation and blush
then with eyeliner draws black tributaries that run purple tears
down the delta of proud high Vietnamese cheekbones

That day long gone, the edge of the mirror
he can't see, now
when he's on stage at Tet, sings
I am Quince, and I am FUNKY
"sexy motherfucker"
he becomes this,
so who is the impersonator?

Turns karaoke at every bar and bowling alley
into an inside-out celebration
of the tornado of hate that swept through him that day,
he doesn't ask
to be your victim,

he sings
groomed whirlwind dervish
does splits with the crack of a wishbone snapped perfect
slaps the mic stand between his palms like a ventriloquist
cracks the air with a dance electric
so bright gotta close his own eyes against his own sexiness
when he sings

lyric-armored son
drunk with dance amore
you wear your purple
you strain moan through lace
you dance through the other side
of your muscles

when people cover their ears at you
you live your life out loud

When it feels like no one
lets you live
at your own volume

You sing.

Vinh and Linda Nguyễn, Again and at Last

Another broken bottle after another girl with no name stepped on your
foot and your hand pancake-flat in a slap too wide hitting only neon air
and another wide-shouldered bouncer with lips clapped shut like two
dominos falling together showing us the door while you scream *fuck
you fuck you get your fucking hands off me fucking*

and here we are, again,

sitting on your fire escape that's wrapped with Christmas lights and
you're smoking and from the street your lit cherry looks like a blinking
star on top of some tree and you're huddled in your ratty blue blanket
with more lint than, well, anything

but isn't this fun?

Remember how we laughed
when you told me about that dude who kissed you
like his tongue was a car wash, exact swirling repetition in your mouth,
wax on wax off, the Mr. Miyagi of Frenching.

Remember the other dude, who you told me
fucked like the secret code to get more men
in Contra, up up down down left right
left right

And another night, like this one, after you convinced me to go
to that fucked-up poetry show
even when I told you I felt like watching spoken word
was like paying five bucks to get punched repeatedly in the face
and say thank you —

I don't know what the big deal with poetry is, anyway —
It's like being drunk, you take too long
to say so little.

We laughed together through all of it even though we knew that these
rough circles of hands and kisses from strangers and too much to drink
always land us back here
on black iron hovering above streets littered with freckles of shining
broken glass
reflecting red and green lights
from Christmas lights you should have taken down a long time ago.

I bring this up now because, we're here again,
you and me, busted up and laughing about other people
talking shit, when we're the ones who got kicked out the club
while shivering in air too cold for the sane,
and liquor makes my tongue do all types of things instead of —

Why can't we just say what we mean?

Like, I want to believe
In Vietnamese American love stories
That haven't been written yet.
Like, your smile is my unlimited, crooked horizon.

Like, I didn't have a standard of beauty
Until I met you.

And I don't want to have to say it, don't want to have to say it,

that these other boys,

the way they love, I mean, both bomb and bomb shelter,
both salve and burn wound on a blister,
both Alcoholics Anonymous and a straight shot of Johnny Walker

I know, you could say the same about me,
I'm no better

I know, when I ask you always say
you want to be loved
not necessarily loved well

I know, but I mean, I mean,
love is like a brick through glass:
first a riot
then fire
then nothing,

I mean couldn't I love you
at least, at least as good as that?

You will ask: why does your poetry
not speak to us of sleep, of the leaves
of the great volcanoes of your native land?

Come and see the blood in the streets,
come and see
the blood in the streets,
come and see the blood
in the streets!
—PABLO NERUDA

Reverse Racism

I'm gonna take every white man from his job and force him to construct light rail transit systems for fifty cents an hour. When they're done I'll make sure they are moved to a special little section of town that we'll call Whiteyville, where tourists can come to shop for curios and eat exotic hot dish. When the American mainstream tongue gets a taste for hot dish, I'm going to open my own fusion hot dish restaurant where I combine hot dish with Asian recipes, and charge people ten times what the food is worth. All the waiters and waitresses will be forced to wear traditional Scandinavian garb. I'll have billboards all over town that say things like "Food as Dull as You Can Get without Being White" and "Our Happy Hour Is as Cheap as a Wayzata White Girl."

I'm going to run for office, promising equality for white men, then when I get elected I'm going to vote against affirmative action for white men, neglect civil liberties for whites, and pass laws that forbid white guys from marrying Asian women. Then I'm going to hit on every single white woman I see and spread rumors about how white guys got small dicks and how white guys are no good for women because they come from such a male-dominated society. White women will tell other white women to marry Asian, because Asian men are the best ones, and they know how to treat women better. I'll exoticize white women and gay white men and desex and demonize all straight white men. Then I'll tell you I don't love white people for the color of their skin, I'm color-blind.

I'm going to teach nothing but Asian American history in every classroom, and when little Morty Crackerman raises his hand and asks *teacher, teacher, we don't study any white people*, I will have him branded as a troublemaker and suspend him from school. Then I will feel a little guilty about it and declare National Whitey Appreciation Week, we'll study the contributions of Kip Winger and Harold Bloom while eating hamburgers and listening to Smashmouth. We will watch the

Honkeytown Crackers play against the Whiteyville Honkies, and in the bleachers we'll do the Wave and the "white men can't dance" dance.

I'm gonna build garbage dumps in white neighborhoods and make sure there's a lot of lead in their water supply. I'll tell my cops to shake down any white guy they see wandering around on the grounds of probable cause and suspicious behavior. Cops will arrest white men just for being white and being outside. Then, I'll deport them. Or maybe I'll beat them down in the street. I'll make sure my Asian friends in the news don't report on it, and if it goes to trial I'll make sure the all-Asian jury and Asian judge pardon me. I'll buy up all the buildings in white neighborhoods and turn them into slums. I will never come around to fix the plumbing, electricity, or take care of the grounds. Then, I will gentrify the neighborhoods and kick white people out.

I'll stick white men in middle-management hell, then put them on a pedestal as an example of how whites can be successful — and urge all whites to work just as hard for just as little. If the Irish and the Italians complain, I'll point at the Scandinavians and say, "look, they're white and they're doing so well! You should be more like them. Then there wouldn't be racism!"

When white men complain, I'll sigh deeply and say, "hey, things are better for you now. You should have tried being around twenty years ago, before me and some other good Asians marched with you white people for your rights. Don't blame me for racism, that stuff happened a long time ago, and anyway, I can't be racist! My girlfriend is white and so are some of my best friends and servants!" Every time a white man fucks up, I'll just shake my head sorrowfully and say, "see?" Then I'll declare that there are too many white men in America, and restrict immigration for white men. The only white men allowed into this country will be the most highly educated white men from Europe: I mean, hey, we need someone to work behind the counter at the gas stations for minimum wage, and who else is gonna drive taxis or run twenty-four-hour grocery stores in the hood?

I'm going on vacation to Europe, with a big-ass backpack, smoking French cigarettes, and asking stupid questions loudly in Vietnamese. I will not shave or take a shower and I'll complain about how dirty Europeans live, then go to those special clubs where white women pay to meet Asian American men. Maybe I'll even marry one of them and take her back with me, but maybe not, cuz I can only have so much luggage and I can always send for a white woman by mail-order later on. Then I'll say, you know, I lived in Europe for a couple of years, so I really know what it's like to be a minority.

I'm gonna start up a shoe company called *Baophi,* (SWOOSH!) and force whites to work in the sweatshops. I will open branches of my fast-food chains and hotels on European soil, I'll mine their lands for uranium and diamonds, I'll drill for their oil, I'll learn their languages and quaint customs, I'll spread my religion, and set up a puppet government full of local corrupt dictators and militaristic tycoons. Then I'll adopt a white child and say, "I saved you, your homeland was so backwards and poor, you would have been eating out of a garbage can in Europe if I didn't save you!"

Of 'course, this may lead to a war. Just to be safe, I'm gonna forcibly remove white American people from their homes because I feel they are a threat to national security. They can stay at the dog-racing tracks until we are sure that they are good and loyal to this country. And while they're gone, I will take everything they ever owned. I will recruit white people to fight against other white people, promising that we'll take care of them if things go wrong, but *if* things go wrong and white people find their way into overcrowded planes and leaky boats to seek refuge in Asian America, I'll turn them away and say "Sorry! No room."

During the war, I will drown my sorrows at dramatically lit bars in Europe. I will win a white prostitute from her evil white pimp in a game of cards. We will have sex, and she will fall in love with me. I will leave her, pregnant, in Europe. When I come back to visit her, she will thrust her baby into my arms and tell me, "please take our child to Asian America, and a better life!" And then she will kill herself. Tragic . . . but good drama! So good, in fact, that I will turn it into a Broadway musical and make a ton of money off of it. Asian actors will put on white makeup and act like white people. You know, I'd love to put real white people in the play, but they're just not talented enough.

I'm gonna make a movie called *White Crush,* about Pacific Islander snowboarders in Minnesota. Then I'm gonna make a movie called *The Last Cowboy,* about a Japanese man who jabs his flagpole into the neck of a white cowboy, then falls in love with the dead man's white wife — after all the white men in the West have been shot to death by Native Americans.

When white men form their own groups to protect themselves, I'll accuse them of being separatists and reverse racists, and force them to let me into their groups. Then I'll cut their budgets because they're really not serving the majority of people. When a white poet gets up to do a poem called "Reverse Racist," I won't get mad, I won't even speak out, because I would have already brainwashed an entire nation of white people to defend us Asians more than they would defend themselves and each other.

Asian Americans are gonna have it all, and white people are going to hate themselves and love us for it. When these white people crumple into a ball, when they try to raise their voices to speak, when they go insane from it all, that's when I'll pat them on the back, and say, that's just the way it is. But we're all human. Don't hate me, it's not my fault, not all of us are like that, don't be like that, don't be a reverse racist.

The Godzilla Sestina

Under the ocean where I was created
in a womb of dancing atoms, a tectonic tale
is breaking the skin of sea floor. Dreams burn here:
lava flows underwater like bleeding fireballs,
sunless sleep disturbed as they listened
for the sound of the nightmares they dropped.

Fat Man and the Little Boy drop,
like two suns tumbling, sent to destroy creation,
no one will be left alive to listen
for the lessons we need to learn from this tale,
just a skyline made of a blossoming fireball
and a symphony of silenced screams horrible beyond hearing.

So I'm born, a radiating thunder lizard, here
to crush American Dreams as my footfalls drop
like apocalypse, and from my lips a chorus of fireballs
razes all that you have created
like runaway rays of sun, my tail
too large to fit in your streets, listen

to see if your superheroes will sing if no one listens,
their words so tired that no one hears,
flag-colored costumes useless in this tale.
Look at the sky for God, for an answer, to see if black rain drops,
to see this towering monster created
by the heat of a million rabid fireballs

unleashed on a people turned to ash by the fire, balled
fists and screams evaporated while history listens.
Now I loom, people scramble in my jagged eclipse, the penumbra I created
is shaped like the ghost of the Enola Gay flying across the moon. Here,
I will illuminate your whispered crimes as the indigo of night drops
before your story is fully told.

Children will sleep trembling under my tail,
the threat of my story like a guillotine of fireballs,
a sharp string of ghastly stars waiting to drop
because even before this lesson, they should have listened,
before we came to this, they should have heard,
they should have known what would be created.

I speak English in this tale, but they don't listen,
so I speak in fireballs, the language they hear,
the nightmare they dropped, the monster they created.

Dear Senator McCain

"I hate the gooks. I will hate them as long as I live."
—JOHN McCAIN, FEBRUARY 17, 2000

"I will call right now, my interrogator that tortured me, a gook. (I can't believe that) anybody doesn't believe these interrogators and prison guards were cruel and sadistic people who deserve the worst appellations possible. . . . Gook is the kindest appellation I can give."
—JOHN McCAIN, FEBRUARY 17, 2000

Dear Senator McCain,

I write this letter on jungle leaves
and the skin of a white man.

I am a gook, a jungle spook,
a steamed apparition
of piss and foot-rot
building torture devices from old rotary phones
and the rusted hulks of American cars

I am that gook, when you turn on the light
I scramble away and if you see me
you know there's ten more
where I came from
catching tracer bullets like fireflies
in my teeth
my language like malaria
sweating itself into your brain

I am a gook, riding on top of water buffaloes,
waving welfare checks like a white flag of surrender

but shot in the back by your finest when they thought
I was standing in a martial arts stance

I am a gook, miscellaneous bomb bait,
Agent Orange evolved primate
creeping thru cash-money-colored jungles
and masturbating neon onto Wall Street
slit eyes fixed on white women
fingers like ten long drips of grease

I am that villain in a white labcoat
trading bomb secrets for red cash
stashing code in surgery-folded eyelids

I am gook, no speak no Engleesh
too much headache, tell me go back to my country,
motherfuck you eh?

I am indeed a gook, polished gold-yellow
at Yale, driving my Ferrari horse-powered dick
deep into your spread-legged streets
while Miss America screams out an orgasmic "there goes the neighborhood"

I am that gook waiting in your nightmare jungle
that gook in front of you with 17 items in the 10 items or less lane at the
        supermarket
that gook born with a grenade in his head
that gook that got a better grade than you in shop class
that gook uppity enuf to stand with his brothers and sisters and demand
        an apology
that gook who patted you on the back and said that's O.K., I hate gooks too

I am that gook who stole your bomb secrets,
that gook that held you hostage,

that gook whose culture your daughter robbed for her tattoos, trinkets,
    and T-shirts
that gook whose language your son attempts to speak so he can crack
    some nookie
from the fortune cookie

I am the gook who blazed you, the gook who saved you

I am gook, chink, slope, slanteye, victor, charlie chan, suzie wong,
    dickless rice picker,
model minority, binder of feet, your favorite sushi waitress, piss-
    colored devil, nip, jap, snow falling on cedars, miss saigon,
    memoir of a geisha, joy luck club, ally mcbeal,

I am gook,
I ate your motherfuckin cat

I am that gook who will hang himself on Nike shoelaces
so your sons and daughters can play pickup
I am that 14 cents an hour gook whose ghosts paint those Gap
    commercials white,
I am that gook that took over your pool hall and your roller rink,
I am this gook, I am that gook, I am your gook, I am my gook
I am that gook, popping out of a motherfuckin bowl of rice
to ask:
Senator
what's the difference
between an Asian
and a gook
to you

Untitled

for Thiên Minh Lý

You could have been my brother.

Thiên Minh Lý, you shared a fraction of my first name,
a vessel of soil from Việt Nam which we were born
to outgrow, uproot, and find once again.
Stabbed two dozen times, and again,
kicked in the head, and again,
by two white men who called you Jap
and bragged about it.

You could have been
the good-looking older brother that everyone liked,
the tennis player and scholar
who loved your awkward younger brother,
sneaking me champagne at the Đà Vũ's,
singing along with the beautiful Ca Sĩ's as they crooned,
making your suit snap in a cha cha or tango,
giving me quarters for Ms. Pac Man.

You could have been my brother, taking care of me
among a throng of your friends
while má and bố were at one of their jobs.
We could have sat, a nightmare platoon, in late-night restaurants,
laughing at white people cuz the only time they dressed as well as us
was for special occasions, like prom, and no matter how hard they tried
they'd never look as good.
Vietnamese and English swarming like angry bees
till we couldn't tell the difference,
putting up with free refills of stank coffee
while daydreaming of cà phê sũ'a đá,

lost between the
white of the salt and the black of the pepper
eating fries and telling ghost stories
while the waiter wishes
we'd just go home.

Thiên Minh Lý, Vietnamese American, honor student,
double major in English and biology, UCLA,
masters in physiology and biophysics in one year at Georgetown,
handsome Vietnamese Student Association leader,
poet who started a Vietnamese newsletter.
Dead.
A red exclamation point in Tustin.
It doesn't matter if they killed you because you were too dark or too bright.
You didn't die for us to learn,
we've learned this lesson many times before.
And no one is talking about you.
They want to bury you twice.

You were my brother, one of many
that I will never meet.
A family of ghosts:
Thanh Mai, Naoki Kamijima, Tony Pham, Won Joon Yoon,
Mukesh and Kanu Patel, Thung Phetakoune,
eight-year-old Jean Kar-Har Fewel's raped body hangs from a North
        Carolina tree.
And then they enlarge our family:
a Hmong home is burnt down in Manitowoc,
Asian women raped and murdered by American GIs in Okinawa, Korea,
by good ole American boys in Spokane, Chicago, Cornell.

My love is burning, slowly, from me
till only a wisp of smoke curls, fills my nostrils,

incense to those who passed
and will pass through me.

To you, Thiên Minh Lý, brother, and all the other brothers and sisters
I never had the chance to love.

Giving My Neighbor a Ride to Her Job

I emerge from 103 at the same time she does from 106.
The hallways full of blondes
whitewashing the walls.
We've never seen this many white people in the building before.
Has gentrification already hit this side of Dale?
Did someone plant a bomb
that exploded with blonde people while we slept?
One of them tells me it's the U of M women's rowing team,
volunteering.
My neighbor asks me for a ride to work, usually her husband
comes home around when she has to leave,
but today he is stranded with a grumpy alternator.
She is Somali. I am Vietnamese. How long have you been here?
Between us this is not offensive. Five years. You? Twenty-six.
She speaks English like my mother.
Her son will speak English like me.
She likes Minnesota.
I don't have the heart to tell her that her son
probably won't.
We don't use the word *refugee*. Somalia, Viet Nam,
both far away, both missed.
In the theaters, *Black Hawk Down* and *We Were Soldiers* play
across whitewashed screens.
One day she will have to tell her son he doesn't have to be like Josh Harnett
to be a hero.
If I ever have a daughter I will have to tell her
that she does not have to love someone the same color as Mel Gibson
to be beautiful.
Words fill my car.
Laughter untranslated.
Languages beautiful.
Together here, we are not broken.

No Offense

The fraternity Delta Tau Delta of the University of Gainesville threw a "Mekong Delta" Party, where the men dressed as American GIs and the women were asked to dress up like Vietnamese prostitutes. They apologized, then threw the same party the following year.

"The real problem is we didn't realize it was wrong," said Charles Emerson, Delta Tau Delta chapter adviser. "It never occurred to us. Otherwise, we would not have done it."

"I'm sorry all of you feel offended," Delta Tau Delta President Ben Davis said. "That was never the intention of the party, and we will never have that party again."

You struck in the same place twice,
igniting homes you call hootch,
twisters of black smoke curl upwards
smogging the glass ceiling

No offense

Globes bought with daddy's credit card
Your clammy hands play cut and paste
with geography, paper dolls on exotic hookers,
puberty hard-on with little white penises limp like struggling flags

No offense

It's okay that you're a bigot cuz your girlfriend is Miss Saigon
and your best friend is the same color as Wesley Snipes
and your affirmative action affection got both of them
through the locked and monitored gates of your neighborhood

No offense
It should be no surprise that stray bullets / civil war /
diseased bamboo stakes / Agent Orange / charred homeland
legless veterans turned beggars / exploited Vietnamese women
is all a big party to you

No offense

Ladies love heroes in uniform, come to liberate them
from foot-binding foes, greased yellow-brown pimps
with your economic downfall at their fingertips
nightmares moving into an American dream's neighborhood

No offense

You wake up from dreams of silk-cocooned prostitutes
send away for exotic mail-order girlfriends
pregnant with assimilation
dying dramatically in your broad(way) arms

No offense

is your only defense.

So lay down your sandbags
like nameless lumped carcasses,
pledge to your brothers
as I will pledge to mine,
because we are coming for you

We are asking Lady Liberty
to take us to America:
we have come to mispronounce your names

Chain your hollow Bruce Lee imitation *hi-yaaaa* to your throat all you want
it won't save you
those Chinese characters on your shirt (which you can't read)
tell me your ass is mine,
that white skin that has meant *individual* and *good guy* and *innocent* and *get
   out of jail free*
will not be honored by us

we will come with gifts of grenades wrapped in banana leaves,
bottles of wine filled with Agent Orange
and a dozen long-stemmed red roses
dipped in napalm.
We have arms made of machetes
and songs that whistle like bullets
through the monsoon

So make yourself dream through beer
and see yourself as an eagle in the mirror;
we will come when you are drunk with yourselves,
we have come to clip the wings of vultures

You wanted a Mekong Delta party

So party on
as your frat house is bombarded
the roof is on fire
the roof is on fire
you will dodge bullets on the dance floor
your parents will be chained to sewing machines
to make your uniforms and costumes
your brothers will turn against you
your sisters will become prostitutes
you will starve
you will get malaria
you will not be able to get a job

tanks will roll into your neighborhood
your children will play with shell casings
in crater-filled suburbs

there will be nothing left

there will be nothing left

No offense.

Called (An Open Letter to Myself)

It was tough for us those times it seemed
our arms braced between not being seen and
the American dream —
raised on Twenty-Sixth and Bloomington slipping through the seams in
    this country's
multiculti quilt
we called it the same old bullshit.

They called us gook, chink, blanket ass, spic, nigger, coon —
(and what was really sad is, we called each other that, too)
went to school and they called us new names: Asian American,
Native American, Latino Latina African American and mixed blood
while still treating us the same damn way and they
called that progress.

We called each other Beaulieu, Saice, Mustafa, Nguyễn —
we talked about hip-hop and minimum wage jobs and
the girls who broke our hearts and they called it
ebonics, broken English, rez accented, pidgin —
we called it talking shit, or man, I was just fuckin witchoo.

We ran in the confused Phillips streets
we ran from the cops, the crazy crackhead motherfuckers,
we ran from our own mothers,
we ran until
our chests burned and our hearts hungered for any place to call home but
we didn't call it running, no, we called it
hangin
we called it, yo what're you doing tonight,
we called it surviving.

So remember those times like when we were sitting around a table
and we heard over the radio about that one kid yeah you remember that kid
who once pulled a knife on you yeah how could you
forget that one kid who chased you down Cedar with a steel bar yeah you
know that one kid who once stuck a loaded gun in your stomach
in that empty candy factory parking lot —
remember when we heard over the radio he got shot dead
in the street
and we didn't know how to feel about it?
And we called that life.

And remember those times when the streetlights ran low
lookin like wingless angels with hazy lazy haloes we
sat in damp basements playing Nintendo listening to
P.E. and De La Soul we would call it
those days

and sometimes we'd turn our stereos up so loud that they'd blow stories
        down
from the trees and we danced in those basements or in those lunchrooms
or in that community center remember where Guillermo and his crew
        airbrushed
a mural about respect we danced a modern-day ghost dance we break-
        danced we salsa'd we cha-cha'd we danced becuz we wanted to
        impersonate the electricity
running through the city
that no one is supposed to dig for
we danced because we had air in our lungs
that we didn't know what to do with
we danced because no one
could
stop us
from dancing.

So when you get out of your fancy college
learning about postracial postmodernist deconstructionist
while still not knowing how to fix your own car
when you're sitting in some Uptown coffee shop
with a poetry book and borrowed powerbook trying to act
like you're not a joke

When you can no longer tell
if you're liberating yourself through expression
or selling your oppression

when they pretend
to listen to you
but still wish you would just
go away
quietly

Remember
there were those of us
living here
who called you
friend.

Bread and Glass

I can't go to those white-bread coffee shops no more.

Slick décor for slick people, so oily they seem to slip through the air,
their breath like boiled milk steam, skin like spoiled cream,
dark coffee circles stained on napkins like snakes eating themselves.

Behind the deli glass are those sandwiches that my mother wakes up at 4 a.m.
to make and wrap, sustenance smeared on focaccia,
wrapped in foggy cellophane.

I look through the glass with the $85,000 postmodern optometrist glasses
that I bought on full scholarship in college,
Viet hood boy made good —
I blink till I can see clearly, and I swear that these white people and white
        wannabes
disappear from all around me,
there is just you and the other Vietnamese, making these bourgeois sandwiches,
gossiping in our secret language,
laughing until your eyes disappear.

The glass is polished by pale hands paid more
than the ones that shaped what's inside of it.
My reflection is a ghost on this glass, a phantom on bread,
my reflection is there and I don't see enough of you in it, mama.

You, whose smile has gotten fuller since you say Buddha has taken
to whispering jokes into your ears,
you who ask me to buy you videos of green destinies,
crouching promises, hidden meanings,
tall, handsome Chow Yun Fat,

so after your two jobs you can come home and
see Asian people fly.

Am I more like these oblivious pale ghosts, so hip they fade chameleon-like
into the atmosphere, who eat without knowing your hands?

All the people who've come to meet
the famous young poet in the house where I was raised,
just around the block where, when I was twelve, I told the kids
I didn't want to run with the Vice Lords because
I'd rather play Dungeons and Dragons —
how nervous they looked,
how they commended you,
impressed that someone so old could live in a neighborhood like this
and raise kids, eyes shifting to shadowed corners
on the watch for cockroaches,
lock the doors of their cars before coming in to eat the food
you spent all day cooking,
the white people you made rich
with the early morning shift of your hands.

How I wanted to tell them this young poet that you admire so much
would be outside jamming a screwdriver into your dashboard
if it weren't for my mother, who wouldn't have to live in the ghetto
if her youngest son just listened to her and became a doctor
instead of a newsworthy poet,
maybe she could afford to move into a neighborhood
that feels safer if they
had one less luxury car,

but at the end of it I
always bite my tongue.
This is my shame.

I take comfort in
my mother's smile, knowing the gift of hands and food cannot be bought,
because when time finally squeezes the light away from us
there will always be the promise of cockroaches in the dark,
fish sauce on formica,
a smell stuck deep beneath your skin
reminding us all of where we come from,

and the lesson that you taught your son, mama:
play dumb to people who are dumber than you,
because glass is thin
and everyone in the world is glass to me —
this is the gift that you passed on,
people can't hide what they truly are no matter how much
they rub,
they can turn on their opaque faces
but I see right through to the other side —

and I wrote this because of the flip side of your gift, Ma,
to always know the right things to say
but speaking the truth anyway.

So I can't go to these white-bread coffee shops no more,
there is just too much glass
and not enough love
for the bread behind it.

For Colored Boys in Danger of Sudden Unexplained Nocturnal Death Syndrome and All the Rest for Whom Considering Suicide Is Not Enuf

I had a dream that we raided
the candy store dumpster on Bloomington,
opened the defective packages,
and had a candy fight
throwing fistfuls of color at each other
while the world waited for us to grow up.

We boys, colored boys, who ran through the streets
with heads spinning, languages spilling into summer
sticking into cracks on sidewalks,
pulling up weeds with our laughter.

Through fits and fights we threw fists,
knocked the pollution in our heads back
and saw the stars,
our noses bleeding like the milky way.

They told us the sky above our heads is the same
but we knew this wasn't true
the first time it rained
batons
we were the only ones getting wet.

Knew we were different because if we stumbled,
drunk and reeling down Franklin,
we'd get a ride in the trunk of a police car
while just a few miles down the same road
white boys drunk off of ten-dollar martinis
were driven home by their tragically beautiful girlfriends.

We hid each other
in the maps of memory:
the garage with a hole in the back
on Fourteenth Avenue
where O_____ scratched his name with a stiletto
or the upturned metal boat in the weedy backyard
on Bloomington
where P_____ hid the *Playboy* he stole from his father.

We, colored boys, who forged our I.D.s
to lie about our age and work for minimum wage
unpacking dirt-kissed vegetables,
rotating dairy products,
working to pay bills that misspelled our names,
saving a little extra for that bus ride to the mall
for one pair of Girbauds and the newest Raiders cap,
pearl-handled switchblades and hidden gats:
we stuck each other up for the things we didn't have.

We were raised to be gentlemen
but did not prefer blondes
(even when our sisters did),
we danced like sparks flying off a downed power line,
bought flowers and tightly rolled horoscopes
while stealing candy from the gas station
for the women who loved missing us
more than loving us

tracing our way through the city
by backtracking the steps to the last dance
with our lovers
learning our way through the city by song

I had a dream that every voice
shattered champagne glasses and bus windows
for the sake of missing us.

Colored boys, who had no rainbows
and even considering suicide was not enough
for men like us, for men like D_____,
who looked for his answers through a noose.
His mother found him, wide-eyed at last,
swaying from the ceiling
like a pendulum from God

or B_____: the only way he could get close to the world
was to jump down from a bridge
to embrace it
like a red-winged angel.
No one came looking for him
so he went to be found.

I had a dream that we never woke up
and the world didn't miss us,
the sons of fathers
who died in their sleep,
hearts trying to keep up with the beating drum
of a land that did not want them dancing.

What happened to their dreams?

Do they live on in us
the sons who have all the heart to feel love
and none of the words to say it

I had a dream
that we told our stories

in sleep
and the demons came
to press on our chests
before we could finish

and the boys, the colored boys of the future,
did not hear the end coming to them,
could only guess when the books would close,
that they wanted to hear how their stories would end
and leaned in close
to our restless sleep
but only heard a failing whisper
of escaping breath,
flavored with dumpster candy and gunpowder

their stories lost to sleep
they could not become men
and none were left
to dream for them.

Yellowbrown Babies for the Revolution

This is *not* about yellowbrown babies for the revolution.

This is *not* about a hand job for my personal-identity-seeking orgasm of
    self-discovery

This is *not* about planting nationalist penis flags into earth mother vaginas

This is *not* about skinning yellowbrown hides so I can make a flag

This is *not* about soy sauce eyes and rice stick thighs

This is *not* about kings or queens, emperors or concubines

This is about love.

This is about laughing in our own language,
the language we can only create together,
the laughter we can create
if we both know what it's like to live without it,
to know we mixed rice with bread
and ate silence,
quietest ingredient in the melting pot,
and we lived on it —

This
is about love,

turning up love's volume till we shake,
till our arms and legs move, till we shout with multiple tongues
and whisper in each other's ears
I will never ask you to change your name
I will never ask you to change your name
your name is at home on my tongue

do you hear me

in this land that wants us blind, deaf, asleep, and defeated
we have to make our own music
because none of these songs have ever been for us,
for the fight inside of us,
pounding fist of the heart against the soul,
the clashing notes inside of our minds,
this is to know what it is like
to have to fight
to love ourselves
this gravity
that sings circular songs in our gut,
we make these songs into homes and we make these homes ours,
there are windows in brown eyes and doors inside of your story
and stairs inside your head and cà phê in your black hair
so let's stay up late,
let's live off of spinning doorknobs,
the thunder of bilingual laughter,
and if we need the night outside to be darker
we'll turn to each other's black hair and lose ourselves there,

and the rain will be pearls,
and blades of lightning will crackle up and down our spines
and we will lift ourselves into the storm

this is about love,
the gradual precipitation that builds to a song, a song that is a storm
        that rides a beat of raindrops on rooftops and city streets and
        makes it look like the stars weep
the love that most will run and hide from
but some
will stand out and risk sickness,

arms wide and head to the sky
because some things must, must soak into our skin

that's the song I need to hear,
that I know I hear,
that lives in my ears

that's the song I know one day will come out right,
that's the song that can't exist
without you

this is the last song on earth,
this is the last song on earth
there is nothing else,
there is nothing else
so fill your lungs
and sing

Sixth Sense

for Juliana Hu Pegues

I.

Salt on silk. And hands through black hair like fingertips walking
    through night grass.
Lake Superior to our knees. And bodies of water to our fathers.
Breath and wind whispering across our cheeks.

II.

Citrus and lilac. And the perfume of flowers trumpeting.
Warm bread. From oven warmth, a home with heat bills paid in full.
Blood and tears. In our noses since birth.

III.

Amuse-bouche — two lips touching, a tongue slips.
Chocolate and orange. Rind on a tongue, burst of velvet.
Essence of lavender lingers long after.

IV.

Bang and crash. Jukebox possessed by your childhood.
Thump and a bump. A car dancing to my upbringing.
Sigh and a whisper. This song I sing.

V.

Yellow. The color of burning clouds singeing a dream.
No, brown. The dirt on our hands and our bellies, full.
Yellow-brown. Both skin, and a sun raw over the earth.

VI.

I mean the darkest days, when our fathers fade and our mothers
fear being left behind. I mean beauty that minnows through concrete
to pop as dandelions waiting
for the pinching fingers of children.
I mean rivers dancing rock, history in the canopy of trees,
I mean the secrets of dogs and cats and I mean
working hands and middle-class daydreams.
I mean broken, I mean fear, and the shiver of not knowing,
I mean in the way that wind holds you
and losing yourself to the vastness of blue water.
I mean you and I
and never asking
what else
is there.

But come here, fear
I am alive and you are so afraid
Of dying.

—JOY HARJO

I feel so poor now.
These words are all I own.

—DAVID MURA

8 (9)

in memory of Fong Lee; and for the Lee family, and the Justice for Fong Lee committee

In 2006, Minneapolis police officer Jason Andersen shot and killed Fong Lee, a nineteen-year-old Hmong American. Andersen was awarded a Medal of Valor, though the Lee family and community members allege that Fong Lee was unarmed and the gun found on the scene was planted by police. During a foot chase in North Minneapolis, Andersen shot at Lee nine times, one bullet missing, the other eight hitting Fong Lee as he ran and as he lay dying on the ground.

1.

Community members point out that accusations about Fong Lee's history and character, specifically allegations that he was in a gang, were allowed in court and written about in the press though there was no proof that Lee was ever involved in a gang. However, none of Officer Andersen's alleged history of abuse or judgments of his character were allowed in court.

One of the devil's greatest powers
is to force you to take a deal
that he himself would never take.

2.

Fong Lee was nineteen *(gang member)*. I can imagine him *(gang member)* and his *(gang member)* family. They are eating *(gang member)* something that steams and it does not steam like food from this *(gang member)* country, the smell lingers *(gang member)* like home. It is Minnesota so *(gang member)* the lights inside no matter how dim somehow make *(gang member)* all indoor rooms feel warm. Now it's summer and he's fishing with his *(gang member)* friends. They *(gang member)* get on bikes and their *(gang member)* legs drape low, *(gang member)*, arms lazy crosses on the handlebars. Their heads lean as they debate the Vikings *(gang member)* and the Twins, slapping absently at the logos *(gang member)* on their caps and *(gang member)* shirts.

93

3.

Officer Jason Andersen *(hero)* shot Hmong American teenager Fong Lee eight times *(to serve and protect)*. A bullet wound in Fong Lee's hand suggests the teenager may have held his hands up in surrender *(decorated officer)* as Officer Andersen *(white)* shot *(Medal of Valor)* him. Andersen was also charged with domestic assault *(peace officer)* by his girlfriend though charges were later dropped *(officer of the law)*. Officer Andersen *(police officer)* was also accused of kicking *(hero)* an African American teenager who was on the ground in handcuffs in 2008.

4.

An all-white jury found Officer Anderson not guilty of using excessive force.

Put a blindfold on me
tell me who you fear
and I will tell you
your skin.

5.

I'm wondering when people will care.
If we made your story into a movie about killing dolphins, perhaps.

6.

I'm eighteen and the brutal cold holsters my hands into the warm solace of my jacket pockets. The police officer snaps his hand to his gun. My pockets are empty. My hands open. Still. My story would have ended in smoke and red snow. If my body lay there, perforated, would I bleed through the holes in his story?

7.

Lost, you turn the car around and see trees stretching up like green-brown fencing up to the blue skies. For a moment you think the woods stretch forever, and somewhere close a bubbling stream whispers white kisses across worn rocks, a deer leans its neck down to drink, the velvet moss of a hushed secret world here in your city. But just beyond the neck of scrub trees is the hint of chain-link, the distant ghost silhouette of strip mall, just one step past the shadows of those leaves are railroad tracks running like stitches over broken glass and gravel.

Minnesota Nice: this city hides its scars well.

8.
All our lives, men with guns.
Chased, in the womb, in the arms
Of our parents.

Our parents
Chased, all our lives,
By men with guns.

In the womb, in our parents' arms
We've run
Chased by men with guns.

(9).
Michael Cho. Cau Thi Bich Tran. John T. Williams.
Tycel Nelson. Oscar Grant. Fong Lee.
May your names be the hymn
wind that sways
police bullets to miss.

Nguyễn in the Promised Land

with thanks to Jane Kim

In another store, in another city, another poem
her last name could be Kim, Mohammed, Rodriguez,
but in this one it's Nguyễn.

In back, a cooler full of beer, cobalt blue ribbons on shining aluminum
and the dairy case her son hated rotating when he was still here,
a little boy, before leaving for training camp
and leaving mother's milk behind
hoping to become a man on the other end of a gun.

Underneath, chipped tiles with flecks of color look like
confetti to the drunks,
looks like faded cheap tile to jaded sober fellow ghetto residents
who take it as evidence
she's yet another vulture, a pirate charging $1.99
for a can of Campbell's.

In front she sits, voices ethereal within the swoon of
Vietnamese operatic music swelling through tinny speakers
of a black boombox
a constellation of cigarettes arrayed above her,
a promise of still-to-light firmament,
sprites of dust fleck Napoleon Dynamite novelty pens
and plastic canisters of bubble gum by the yard.

She props her head up above lottery tickets, a rough patchwork quilt of
     scratch-offs beneath her elbows,

She's heard it all before,

"Miss NU-YEN, pray for me, if I win the lottery
I can finally get my alternator replaced,

Buy a nice house and raise my kids somewhere quiet,

Hire a lawyer and sue that son of a bitch like he deserves,

Miss NU-YEN, your name rhymes with win, it's a good sign,
pray for me and if I hit those numbers I'll come back
and give you some of the money —"

She smiles, waves her arm, doesn't have the heart or patience
to teach them how to actually pronounce her name,
doesn't think any of them will ever win,
and she doesn't pray.

But she wishes them luck all the same; she just doesn't wait for it.

Unlucky is not knowing where her husband is.
True, the communists might have gotten him in the motherland,
or maybe he just ran off with someone
whose hair was a bit longer, teeth a bit straighter,
who's to say.

Unlucky is being held up more than twelve times at gunpoint over
the years, men assuming they all look alike to her
but still they wear masks —
she sees and remembers their knuckles, tight and tense near the trigger.

Let them drain her twelve-hour days of diabetes-flavored candy bars and
        small stories
filled with prayer and slow menthol death and go back to where you came
from you gook bitch in exchange for shivering aftermath with empty pockets,
an apathetic visit from police hours later,

and a chance to kickstart this shit all over again
the next morning.

That's it.

And she's never bought a gun.

Mom's not a hero either. Depending on who she hates that day
she tells the police that all blacks, Chicanos, Hmong, Indians,
even Vietnamese, are no good and are out to get her.

Her daughter went to college on the dimes spun in this store,
has marched for Mumia and for the rights of the working class
tells her mom it's not right to be racist, that calling the cops on her
fellow ghetto residents is counterrevolutionary —
we people of color have to stick together, she says.

Why doesn't anyone ever say that
to the men holding guns?

But her kids don't understand Vietnamese well enough to comprehend,

a mom doing her best with what she's got

a merchant of cigarette-flavored death
dreams the bubble of bottled soda exploding
and the smell of a wet beer kiss

bread and soup too expensive for her to be declared
slant-eyed Jesus of the ghetto

lottery tickets fat with long promises
just beneath her reach.

Everyday People

It's one of those nights when no one wants to be Asian.
They want to slip into something easier.

Any city, any bar, where there's a mixer or social event designed
to put a bunch of Asians in one room
and hope they don't hate each other's guts.

He is already there, back stiff from work,
already made small talk with the sea of political consultants,
paralegals, actors, nonprofit arts administrators, and community workers,
almost everyone dressed in a neat flat black.

She enters, and she is herself. She lets out a small sigh
that says
I hate this shit but I love my people.
She feels awkward not wearing black,
doesn't know many of these people, doesn't feel she's a part
of their income bracket, does not watch *Sex and the City* so
she doesn't know what to talk about with whom.

He looks closer as she walks by — their eyes meet.
They introduce themselves. They are both Nguyễns.

She works for the community. He's an investment banker.
It happens suddenly

they both look each other in the eye:

He sees that he doesn't have a chance
with someone usually entranced by blue eyes
one of those expensive-tea-and-gentrified-hardwood-floor types of girls
with a bathroom full of fruit extracts and verbena

and soap bars with oatmeal sticking out of them
so visitors mistake washing their hands for breakfast.
She's probably got
an amazing vinyl collection of R&B, soul, and
old-school hip-hop
and a white underground rapper boyfriend
with lots of tattoos.

Yeah he says to himself she is probably a poet
who takes her shoes off before she gets on stage
for some fucking reason,
probably only likes boho / spoken word / poet types of boys / who
nod their heads when she speaks of oppression
nod their heads so fierce to her didactic
that they make her feel like hip-hop.
She probably hates me for making money
materialistic, she'll hiss
but the money she spends on Paulo Freire books, rare vinyl,
and tattoos could support an entire village back in Viet Nam.

Yes he thinks these things
but he doesn't ask her.

If he did, maybe she would tell him
about a man put into a reeducation camp in Viet Nam,
his pregnant wife unable to sleep because she was afraid
she would see her husband in nightmares.
All they had, a little money in a tea tin,
they escaped.
Born on a leaky boat, miles away from shore.
Raised in America, on a tiny farm
the only Vietnamese among Hmong farmers.
Her parents said she was a gift from heaven
to survive being born on that boat
they gave her raw cucumbers, they gave her stories,

they gave her everything they could,
and she would secretly bury pennies in a corner,
water them every day
to see if she could make them grow —
a tree with spinning copper fruit.

If he asked maybe she would tell him
that in this hurried city, sometimes she misses that farm,
the pond where she skinned frogs and skinned knees
and skimmed the face of the water with her feet as she swang from trees.

But her parents wanted her to go to school in the city,
where the same whiteboy who called her a chink in high school
asked her to have a cup of coffee with him
and the white women
wanted to show her pictures of their trips to India.
At times she just wanted to get away
from the two jobs and the schoolwork
and stare at the moon's reflection
unraveling itself on the Mississippi,
every wave breaking it apart
and bringing it back together again
as if it were a ball of silver threads
that couldn't decide if it wanted to be
solidly itself
or become undone,
wondering if the people on that leaking boat
saw the moon like she did
and wondered who was buried under it
so she could be alive.

She would tell him
that her parents still send her
dried fruit, pickles they jar themselves
and when she opens the box

she sits at her chipped kitchen table
and cries
wondering why she can't send them more money,
see them more often,
why they refuse to hate
their beautiful baby girl.

Maybe she would say that she doesn't move
in mysterious ways;
these are mysterious days when being yourself
is harder than being someone else.

So who is he to judge her,
this man-child with the expensive sweater
who probably lives with his mother,
drives an Acura like he would drive his little Asian dick,
drinks too much, plays Texas hold 'em all night
and shouts too loud when he loses,
plays basketball
badly
with his former *Azyn Pride* friends
who hide their tattoos under long-sleeved shirts.
Who is he to judge me? He probably
can't dance, can't hold a conversation
for more than fifteen minutes,
his entire wardrobe from two stores: Banana Republic
and Armani Exchange.
He has no personality
and blames the reason he can't get a date
on Asian women dating white dudes

so who is he to judge me? she thinks
but doesn't ask him.

If she did, maybe he would tell her
that when he was a boy, his mother
stepped on a land mine, it opened beneath her
like a thirsty flower unfolding,
his mother suddenly becoming
a million red broken stars
falling.
His auntie, dead from giving birth
to an Agent Orange baby
twisted to death in the womb.

Another auntie, who survived but was trapped when the communists came —
his father spent days at the factory, overtime, weekends,
asking his senile father to look after his boys,
sent money to auntie, did paperwork and kept appointments
with immigration authorities who could care less
about another gook —

but his daddy got her to America
and she spit in his face in the airport
blamed him for leaving them back in Viet Nam
to starve and suffer.

How he saw this all and swore
he would make enough money
to never see that look on his father's face again
the look when his uncle
stumbled in to borrow money for liquor and gambling,
how kids in the neighborhood laughed at him
when they bought canned soup and macaroni
with food stamps.
Now he's an investment banker, living in a tiny apartment
sending money to his relatives, in America and Viet Nam,
stopped hanging out with his friends

who kept asking him where all his money went.
Sometimes he sits alone
and holds his cold phone to his ear
pretends its silence is his mother,
what her voice would be like, asking him
if he had eaten, if he was taking care of himself,
if he had found a nice Vietnamese girl.
How his father sat him down before he left
and said you have my blood in you
which means you will never be beautiful
but you will always survive.

He may have told her these things
if she had asked.

She may have listened, if he would
have let her.

She may have wanted to tell all,
he may have wanted to hear as much about her
as she was willing to say.

But neither asks,
not one, not the other.

So they pass, two leaking ships
trying to stay afloat
clinging tight
to what they know.

Race

with thanks to Tim Hong and Brooke Choo

Huey Tran and JPEG Nguyễn were the two best street racers in Frogtown
(even though they shared a car
cuz goddammit that shit was expensive),
JPEG's family was almost middle class —
Huey's wasn't —
so although it was really JPEG's Celica,
Huey was the better racer and better mechanic,
and he could make that car sing on the road,
boy,
sing so loud they called it Linda Trang Dai.

JPEG's real name was Nimoy cuz his parents
came to America and watched *Star Trek* and
thought Nimoy was an American name —
nowadays he called himself JPEG because he thought he was

SO

PRETTAY

but Huey called him Nimoy which bugged him but hey
what are you gonna do.

So one Saturday night they heard the whiteboy wanted to race them.
Whiteboy's real name was Todd Landers but everyone called him
Whiteboy or Poseur or Fuckhead cuz though he spent hella money
souping up his Ford Focus most of that shit was cosmetic —
like the spoiler that he carefully painted to match the paint job,
a gigantic fin sticking up from the back roof
like a whale's tail stapled to a guppie.

Some called Whiteboy the Mandarin behind laughing teeth
cuz he had

kanji tattoos on his arms he thought said
Strength in love but really said something more like
Unreliable delivery service
and he wore a purple satin jacket with dragons and phoenix all over it
which made it look like Confucius threw up on him
after an all-night drinking binge.

Anyway he wanted to race Huey and JPEG for pink slips
which was fucking stupid cuz they didn't want his car anyway
and no one really races for their cars
unless they have a Hollywood contract
but Whiteboy wanted to race and he said if he won
he would get some free tune-ups from Huey and if Huey won —

Well, what?

Huey thought about it and said if I win, you give me that
wack-ass purple jacket you wear all the time,
and Whiteboy laughed and said *uh O.K. bro*

Huey called his girl Vina who borrowed the car earlier
to take her dad to INS for some bullshit paperwork
(Asian people you know how they do us)
and Huey and JPEG didn't need the car that day anyway
since they both had the day off from the garage,
business had been slow since
most "real Americans" wanted their "real American cars"
to be fixed up by "real Americans"—
so they were just gonna hang out and play Gran Turismo all day.
Vina drove over to Huey's place with the yellow Celica
screeching the tires as she pulled up to the curb,
which made JPEG say goddamn I think sometimes
she drives that car faster than you.

And they all hopped in and drove over to Snelling and Ford Parkway
and Vina remembered to take her pink Hello Kitty pencil case
from the glove compartment that held her .22.
See, her mom got her the gun when she went off to college
cuz she heard those crazy white frat boys be raping women all the time,
and figured if her daughter wanted to go so far away for college
she should have some protection.
So Vina's mom, tough country girl
from Thái Bình, went next door to the café where all the Viet hoodlums
drank coffee and played cards
and asked one of them to buy her a gun for her baby girl.
When she first got the gun Vina took out the dividers inside the pink Hello
Kitty pencil case
to put the .22 in (perfect fit!) and had been carrying it
around
since college cuz some habits are hard to break.

JPEG told her to take the gat out of the glove compartment
cuz it would just weigh the car down as they rolled up
and saw that a small group
of people had come through to watch the race.

And they saw that Whiteboy was wearing his purple mandarin jacket
and he said there's nothing on under this cuz I'm gonna win,
and Vina said if you let that whiteboy win I'm never gonna speak
to you again,
and JPEG said why don't you just shoot him in the foot, Vina, which
will undoubtedly affect his acceleration abilities,
and Huey got out of the car and said hey what up Jarvis,
and the whiteboy said my name's not Jarvis,
and Huey said my bad, all you white guys look alike to me.

And the crew that had gathered to watch were mostly Asians
though it had enough different colors to be a Benetton ad
and Vina said they should all hold hands and sing "We Are the
World" together

It was decided that Huey would race against the whiteboy
so about half the crowd stayed at the starting line and half drove
down to the finish line. Huey got behind the
wheel of the Celica and Whiteboy got into his Focus with the
big fakey-looking spoiler and the kanji stickers that he thought
said *Fast and Furious* but really said
Szechuan Chicken
and with a wave from Vina they were off

Into

FIRST GEAR
And Huey was feeling pretty good cuz

SECOND GEAR
Fuckhead Mandarin Whiteboy was already kinda behind
and Huey knew that he was gonna mess up shifting into

THIRD GEAR
and everything is getting faster now and Huey starts getting
excited
because although at first he thought beating this fool in this
race was
going to be more like punching the clock he was starting to
feel it a little bit,
want it just
a little bit,
especially as he shifted into

FOURTH GEAR

and the engine purrs like a cat with speed
mixed into its Meow Mix and the hum starts thrumming from
the wheels to the top of his head and the wind starts making
waves around the windshield of the Celica and he starts
worrying about cops and he starts laughing a little bit as he shifts into

FIFTH GEAR

and Huey swears to God the spoiler is a sail as he
slithers down the sleek roads wet with neon perspiration and
the streetlights are whizzing by so fast they look like
they're ping-pong balls popping off the table of the horizon
and he gets a little scared now scared enough to laugh a little
more and that whiteboy wannabe wankster waste is so far
behind he can't even dream of catching up

SIXTH GEAR

and his head is spinning like a globe and his eyes are
like the finger that'll stop it when looking for home and every pock
on the tar is caressed like pores on a lover's face by this car
he spends hours on in its maze of tubes and wires trying
to learn its secret language trying to get it to laugh and go
just a little bit faster now its only direction is forward like
a dancer snap-launched from a slingshot and the night
sky is doing that *Star Wars* Millennium Falcon thing and he
wonders if JPEG will let him call him Chewbacca which
makes him laugh even harder and the other cars and the city
lights and the dandelions stick up like sunflowers from
the boulevard streak past air blowing against the Celica like
a warning breath life flashing in front of the headlights like
kids in Sai Gon on a Sunday on their mopeds all cool glares
and upturned chins and cigarette ash and SARS-blocking facemasks

and it's all over. A few seconds later Whiteboy
Fuckhead Jarvis Mandarin's car crosses the finish line and
he gets out asking if they're really gonna take his jacket.

Huey says, hand it over.

Motherfucker, JPEG adds.

And then Huey, Vina, and JPEG,
young, beautiful, and Vietnamese,
walked back toward their car, not knowing where they were
going
but knowing they would get there together
and as they were about to get into the Celica
Vina turned to their pale defeated opponent
because Vietnamese women always got to get the last word
and said
in case you haven't noticed,
this was all a
Race
and you lost.

Acknowledgments

I owe thanks to a tremendous amount of people. Teachers, professors, friends, people who gave me opportunities, advice, came to a show, gave me a ride to the airport. Asian American spoken word artists and community members — you all are like family to me. There are far too many people to name, it'd be another book. Please take this thank you, and forgive me if I didn't thank you by name.

Thanks to everyone at Coffee House, especially Allan Kornblum, Chris Fischbach, and Jessica Deutsch. I thought I'd be dead before I'd see the day my poems were published in my own book — thank you for this.

Thanks to David Mura, who along with Allan and my partner, Juliana, deserves the most praise for convincing me that Coffee House was not trying to trick me when they asked for my manuscript. Without those three people, this book would not exist.

Special thanks to Tony Nguyễn for proofing and advising on the Vietnamese tones, names, and grammar for this book, and Binh Danh for the amazing cover art.

Esther Torii Suzuki and Vijit Ramchandani, Don Belton, Gabe and Jesse — rest in peace.

Thanks to the Phi/Nguyễn family and the Hu Pegues family. Thanks to everyone at the Loft Literary Center, especially Jerod Santek. Thanks to the Minnesota State Arts Board, SASE/Intermedia Arts, Asian American Renaissance, Theater Mu, Pangea, Patrick's Cabaret, Kieran's Irish Pub, and the Minnesota Slam teams. And thanks to the Fong Lee family and the Justice for Fong Lee committee.

Special thanks to Stephen Bor, Sahra Nguyễn, Jennii Le, Theresa Vu, Derek Kan, Jane Kim, Siwaraya Rochanahusdin, Taiyo Na, Steve Morozumi, Momo Chang, Jay Tsukamoto, Sham-e-Ali Nayeem, Robert Karimi, Christy NaMee Eriksen, Mikari Suzuki, Rodrigo Sanchez Chavarria, Kai Ma, Rush and Vashion Merchant, Larry Lucio Jr., Toki Wright, Thi Nguyễn, Kathy Haddad, Mahnaz Kousha, Diane Glancy, Janet Pablo, Danny "Dandiggity" Le, Anida Yoeu Ali, Lisa Washington, Dan S. Le, Emmanuel Ortiz, Ravi Chandra, Asia Continental, Helen Yum, Chamindika Wanduragala, Pradeepa Jeeva, Marcie Rendon, Mark Anthony Rolo, Diego Vazquez, Jr., Carolyn Holbrook, Toby Folwick, Frank Sentwali, Tou Saiko Lee, Katie Ka Vang, May Lee-Yang, Mai Neng Moua, Blong Yang, Lac Su, Dipankar Mukherjee, Meena Natajarian, Kayva Yang, Emily Chang, Hei Kyong Kim, Su-Yoon Ko, Eva Song Margolis, Michelle Myers, Catzie Vilayphonh, Marlon Esguerra, Charissa Uemura, Regie Cabico, Brandon Lacy Campos, Geo, Beau Sia, Kelly Tsai, Marion Gomez, Marisa Carr, Tish Jones, Nguyễn Qui Duc, Isabelle Thuy Pelaud, Yen Le Espiritu, Elaine Kim, Leah Lakshmi Piepzna-Samarasinha, Jenny Assef, Leilani Ly-huong Nguyễn, George Suzuki, Anmol Chaddha, Yuri Kochiyama, Eddie Zheng, Viet Mike Ngo, Peter Rachleff, Li-Young Lee, Sun Mee Chomet, Linda Nguyễn, Stevie Peace, Janet Carlson, Duchess Harris, Ruth Burks, Rose Chu, Karen Lucas, Laurie Carlos, Barrie Jean Borich, Linnea Stenson, Ananya Chatterjea, David Kaminsky, the Pine family, Cullen Bailey Burns, E. G. Bailey, Shá Cage, Tom Borrup, Patrick Scully, Jody Koizumi, Valerie Lee, Tom Horgen, Faith and Lym-sung Kim, Nomi, Shaggy Flores, Celine Liu, Taylur Thu Hien Ngo, Rebekah Linh Collins, Barbara Tran, Rich and Heewon Lee, Antonio Rosario,

Billy Collins, Paul Lai, Shannon Gibney, Greg and Cathy Choy, Sarah Agaton Howes, Kurt Kwon, Kiwi, Mike Hoyt, Katie Leo, Jojo Gaon, Nancy Yap, Ryan Suda, Daren Mooko, Kay Barrett, Allisonjoy Faelnar, Jimmy Tran, Janet S. Kim, Joy Gloria Liu, Bambu, Jona Mercado Caberto, Malaya Arevalo, Ishle Park, Maya Santos, Francis Hwang, Lori Young-Williams, Wing Young Huie, Jae Ran Kim, Sun Yung Shin, D'Lo, Vinh Hua, YaliniDream, Keith Chow, Jerry Ma, Jeff Chang, Hsindy Chen, Steve Lin, Vudoo Soul, Saymoukda Vongsay, Walidah Imarisha, Turiya Autry, Chris Tsou, Sarwat Rumi, Guante, Justin Woo, Emily Lawsin, Proletariat Bronze, Bert Wang, Sherry Quan Lee, Ricardo Levins Morales, Louis Alemayehu, Paul S. Flores, Olga Garcia, Craig Perez, Bassey Ikpi, Bhurin Said and all the Silk Mangos.

Above and beyond, thanks to Thuyet Nguyễn, Alicia Tran, Giles Li, Tatiana Ormaza, Dennis Kim, Douglas and Nicole Kearney, Darren Lee, Jasmine Kar Tang, Heather Wang, Tony Nguyễn, Ed Bok Lee, Sajin Kwok, and Lisa Ellingson.

And last but not least, thank you to Juliana Hu Pegues and Sông Mikiko Haley Phi-Hu, for making it all worth it.

Colophon

Sông I Sing was designed at Coffee House Press, in the historic
Grain Belt Brewery's Bottling House near downtown Minneapolis.
The text is set in Fournier.

Funder Acknowledgments

Coffee House Press is an independent nonprofit literary publisher. Our books are made possible through the generous support of grants and gifts from many foundations, corporate giving programs, and through donations from individuals who believe in the transformational power of literature. Coffee House Press receives major operating support from the Bush Foundation, the Jerome Foundation, the McKnight Foundation, and from Target. Coffee House also receives support from: three anonymous donors; Elmer L. and Eleanor J. Andersen Foundation; Around Town Literary Media Guides; Patricia Beithon; Bill Berkson; the James L. and Nancy J. Bildner Foundation; the E. Thomas Binger and Rebecca Rand Fund of the Minneapolis Foundation; the Patrick and Aimee Butler Family Foundation; the Buuck Family Foundation; Ruth and Bruce Dayton; Dorsey & Whitney, LLP; Fredrikson & Byron, P.A.; Sally French; Jennifer Haugh; Anselm Hollo and Jane Dalrymple-Hollo; Jeffrey Hom; Stephen and Isabel Keating; the Kenneth Koch Literary Estate; the Lenfestey Family Foundation; Ethan J. Litman; Mary McDermid; Sjur Midness and Briar Andresen; the Rehael Fund of the Minneapolis Foundation; Deborah Reynolds; Schwegman, Lundberg & Woessner, P.A.; John Sjoberg; David Smith; Mary Strand and Tom Fraser; Jeffrey Sugerman; Patricia Tilton; the Archie D. & Bertha H. Walker Foundation; Stu Wilson and Mel Barker; the Woessner Freeman Family Foundation; and many other generous individual donors.

TARGET.

To you and our many readers across the country,
we send our thanks for your continuing support.

Good books are brewing at www.coffeehousepress.org